Magic, Myth, and Mystery

KRAKEN

DO YOU BELIEVE?

This series features creatures that excite our minds. They're magical. They're mythical. They're mysterious. They're also not real. They live in our stories. They're brought to life by our imaginations. Facts about these creatures are based on folklore, legends, and beliefs. We have a rich history of believing in the impossible. But these creatures only live in fantasies and dreams. Monsters do not live under our beds. They live in our heads!

45th Parallel Press

Published in the United States of America by Cherry Lake Publishing
Ann Arbor, Michigan
www.cherrylakepublishing.com

Reading Adviser: Marla Conn MS, Ed., Literacy specialist, Read-Ability, Inc.
Book Design: Felicia Macheske

Photo Credits: © Blueguy/Shutterstock.com, cover; © Kei Shooting/Shutterstock.com, cover; © zhengzaishuru/Shutterstock.com, cover, 1, 12; © Ethan Daniels/Shutterstock.com, 5; © Unholy Vault Designs/Shutterstock.com, 7; © stjepann/Shutterstock.com, 8; © Ysbrand Cosijn/Shutterstock.com, 11; © Dudarev Mikhail/Shutterstock.com, 12; © Balasioiu Sorin Ionut/Shutterstock.com, 15; © Wallenrock/Shutterstock.com, 17; © Dario Sabljak/Shutterstock.com, 18; © HWitte/Shutterstock.com, 21; © Catmando/Shutterstock.com, 22; © musicman/Shutterstock.com, 24; © OSORIOartist/Shutterstock.com, 27; © carlosramos1946/Shutterstock.com, 29

Graphic Elements Throughout: © denniro/Shutterstock.com; © Libellule/Shutterstock.com; © sociologas/Shutterstock.com; © paprika/Shutterstock.com; © ilolab/Shutterstock.com; © Bruce Rolff/Shutterstock.com

45th Parallel Press is an imprint of Cherry Lake Publishing.

Library of Congress Cataloging-in-Publication Data

Names: Loh-Hagan, Virginia, author. | Loh-Hagan, Virginia. Magic, myth, and mystery.
Title: Kraken / by Virginia Loh-Hagan.
Description: Ann Arbor, Michigan : Cherry Lake Publishing, [2017] | Series: Magic, myth, and mystery | Includes bibliographical references and index.
Identifiers: LCCN 2016031786| ISBN 9781634721486 (hardcover) | ISBN 9781634722803 (pbk.) | ISBN 9781634722148 (pdf) | ISBN 9781634723466 (ebook)
Subjects: LCSH: Kraken—Juvenile literature. | Sea monsters—Juvenile literature. | Animals, Mythical—Juvenile literature.
Classification: LCC QL89.2.K73 L64 2017 | DDC 001.944—dc23
LC record available at https://lccn.loc.gov/2016031786

Cherry Lake Publishing would like to acknowledge the work of The Partnership for 21st Century Skills. Please visit *www.p21.org* for more information.

Printed in the United States of America
Corporate Graphics

TABLE of CONTENTS

Chapter One

The Monster of Sea Monsters

What does Kraken look like? Where does it live? How does it hunt?

"Release the Kraken!" Kraken is a sea monster. It's the largest imagined by mankind. There's little known about it. Kraken is very rare. It's hardly ever seen. Most people believe there's only one Kraken.

Kraken is half-squid. It's half-crab. It has a scary **maw**. A maw is a beast's mouth and jaws. Its maw has many rows of teeth. The teeth are 5 feet (1.5 meters) long. Its maw can open really wide. It has a beak. The beak is sharp. It can shatter anything.

Kraken belongs to the cephalopod family.
Cephalopods include octopuses, squids, and cuttlefish.

Explained by Science!

Sailors saw bubbles. They saw dangerous waves. They saw new land. They thought these were signs of Kraken. Scientists say these were signs of underwater volcanic activity. Volcanoes are common in Iceland, where Kraken lives. Gas bubbles stir up the sea. Poisonous gases rise up. Iceland has 30 active volcano systems. Thirteen have erupted since the year 874. Iceland is located over a hot spot. It's on the mid-Atlantic Ridge. This means it's over a crack in the ocean floor. The plates rub against each other. They slide in opposite directions. They push each other up and down. When they separate, they release lava. The lava goes to the surface. It cools down. It forms new land. Sailors believed these new islands were Kraken. Iceland has a big volcanic event once every five years.

Kraken is over a mile long. It's the size of 10 ships. It has 12 **tentacles**. Tentacles are long, moving arms. They have over 1,000 sucking cups on them. The suckers have tiny teeth. The teeth look like spikes. The tentacles have big claws at the end. The tentacles are huge. They reach the top of tall ships. They come out of Kraken's sides.

Kraken is a Scandinavian word. It means an unhealthy animal. It also means something twisted. Kraken comes from a German word, too. The word is *krake*. It means octopus.

Kraken can destroy ships easily.

Kraken lives in deep northern oceans. It lives in caves. It uses its tentacles to **anchor** itself. It sticks to the ground. It crawls along the ocean floor.

Kraken hunts at night. It eats anything that comes by. It stretches its neck. It burps. It **vomits** food. Vomit means to throw up. It poops. All kinds of guts come out. It uses its guts as bait. Sea creatures love to eat Kraken waste. They come to feed. Kraken lets sea creatures enter its maw. It locks its jaws. It chews and swallows.

Kraken stays deep in the ocean. But sometimes it surfaces. It's disturbed by passing ships. It craves human flesh.

Kraken mainly lives around Norway, Iceland, and Greenland.

Chapter Two

Sailors, Beware!

How does Kraken attack? How does it trick sailors? What are its skills?

Kraken emerges from the ocean depths. It attacks ships. It wraps its big tentacles around ships. It **capsizes** ships. Capsize means to turn over. Sailors fall out. They hit the water. Kraken's smaller tentacles grab sailors. Kraken uses its beak to eat sailors. It stuffs sailors into its maw. It pulls ships to the bottom. It sinks ships. It drowns sailors. Kraken saves them to eat later.

Kraken chases fish. Fishermen follow the fish, too. Kraken traps fishermen and their boats. Kraken sneaks up. It attacks. It goes back underwater. This makes waves. The waves make a **whirlpool**. Whirlpools are like hurricanes in the water. Whirlpools can trap and sink ships miles away.

When fishermen catch a lot of fish, they say to each other, "You must have fished on Kraken."

Kraken has many tricks. It can **camouflage** itself. It blends into its surroundings. It changes colors. It changes to red, green, or orange. It's hard to see Kraken underwater.

It can also disguise itself as an island. Sailors think they see land. They sail toward Kraken. They try to land on it. Then, Kraken attacks. It raises its tentacles. It drags them down.

Sailors get tricked by calm waters. They think they're safe. Kraken makes bubbles. The bubbles make dangerous waves. Sailors don't notice in time. They can't escape. Kraken is quick.

Kraken has a large brain. It is smart.

When Fantasy Meets Reality!

Some people think Kraken may have been a colossal squid. Colossal squids are bigger than giant squids. They're 40 to 50 feet (12 to 15 m) long. They weigh 1,650 pounds (748 kilograms). They're the largest known animals without a spine. The sucking cups on their tentacles have sharp hooks. The hooks spin and move. Giant squids have teeth on their sucking cups instead. Colossal squid bodies are wider and stouter than giant squids. They have longer bodies. They have shorter tentacles. They have larger beaks. They attack slowly. They surprise their prey. They also like really cold waters. But they live in oceans close to Antarctica. Kraken lives in northern oceans.

Kraken's suckers are strong. They can pull the flesh away from bones.

Kraken has many skills. It's fast. It moves at a high speed. It uses jets of water. It launches itself through water. It's a powerful swimmer. It swims in circles around ships. This traps ships.

It leaves behind black oil. This blinds prey. Its spit has poison. It doesn't have bones. It pulls itself through tight spots. It's strong. It has big eyes. It sees well. It can see in total darkness. It can see far away.

Chapter Three

Cracking the Kraken

What stops Kraken from killing all the time? What are its limitations? Why is Kraken safe from harm?

Kraken doesn't have magical powers. Its power is its big size and strength. Magic also doesn't affect Kraken. Humans can't control it. Nobody can control it. Nobody escapes. Nobody survives a Kraken attack.

It's hard to stop Kraken. Luckily, Kraken stops itself. It doesn't need to eat humans all the time. It rests after attacking ships. It's satisfied for a while. It can live off sea creatures. It doesn't need to surface much.

It can be killed. It feels pain. Bombs are the best way to hurt it. But no one can find it. This makes Kraken safe.

Monster hunters have tried to trap Kraken. They've failed.

Kraken doesn't make itself easy to kill. It hides. It stays safe.

Kraken can't leave the water. It'll die on land.

Sometimes, it loses body parts during an attack. It can lose tentacles. It can lose arms. But it can regrow body parts. The new parts are soft. They're not strong yet. This makes Kraken weak. So it hides. It doesn't come out.

It has one **predator**. Predators are hunters. Sperm whales would like to eat Kraken. But they can't find it. Dead sperm whales wash to shore. Scientists found scars on the whales' skin. They think Kraken's tentacles slashed at the whales.

SURVIVAL TIPS!

- Don't take boat trips out in the far ocean. Take boat trips in smaller bodies of water. Stay close to land. If you can see the shore, you might be okay. Definitely don't take boat trips in northern Europe.

- Avoid large schools of fish. Remember, fish travel in front of Kraken.

- Stay away from large patches of bubbling waters. This might be a sign of Kraken. Calm seas don't bubble.

- Get a submarine. Load it with weapons. Small, quick submarines are best. They're easier to move around. You want to quickly get in and out. Add electricity to the front of the submarine. This way, you can shock Kraken.

Chapter Four

Mysterious Beginnings

Why don't we know about Kraken's origins? How are Kraken and giants squids connected? Why is Kraken so huge?

Nobody knows how Kraken came to be. Kraken is mysterious. It's only seen when it wants to be seen. There are different stories about Kraken's **origins**. Origins are beginnings.

Some say Kraken has been around for a long time. It was born when the world was made. It will live until the world ends.

Some people think a mad wizard made Kraken. Some people think Kraken was created to scare people from traveling on the seas.

Kraken has been able to live a long time because nobody can kill it.

Scientists think Kraken is a giant squid. Sailors didn't know much about animals. They thought giant squids were monsters. Giant squids and Kraken are similar.

Giant squids are 40 feet (12 m) long. They have eight arms. They have two long feeding tentacles. They live in the deep ocean. They can see in the dark. They have special eyes. They track fish. They shoot out their tentacles. They pull in their prey. They use their beaks to crush prey. They use their tongues to eat. Their tongues have small teeth. They move slowly. They use jet power to move fast.

Kraken stories may have started because of sailors' fears of the unknown.

Know the Lingo!

- **Architeuthidae:** family consisting of eight species of giant squid
- **Carpus:** wrist part of the tentacle
- **Dactylus:** finger part of the tentacle
- **Davy Jones' locker:** bottom of the sea where drowned sailors and ships sink
- **Dogs running before their master:** heavy waves before a big hurricane
- **Grotto:** cave
- **Leviathan:** sea monster referenced in the Old Testament
- **Manus:** hand part of the tentacle
- **Mariner:** sailor
- **Pig boat:** submarine
- **Radula:** tongue with small teeth
- **Squidzilla:** giant sea monster
- **Statocyst:** organ used to sense orientation and motion in water

Kraken rarely leaves the deep ocean. Deep-sea living makes animals big. Temperatures are cold. This increases size. This also increases **life span**. Life span is how long something lives. Kraken continues to grow. It doesn't stop growing. This means it keeps getting bigger. It lives a long time.

In 1735, **botanist** Carl Linnaeus made a list of animals. A botanist studies plant life. He included Kraken in his list. But there's no proof of Kraken's existence. There were only sailors' stories. So Linnaeus took Kraken off his list. Kraken is a mystery.

"Deep-sea gigantism" is the phenomenon of deep-sea animals growing to giant sizes.

Chapter Five

Kraken vs. Vikings

What are other versions of Kraken? How are Kraken and Norse people connected?

Pliny the Elder was an ancient Roman scientist. He referred to Kraken's danger. He said, "No animal is more **savage** in causing the death of a man in the water." Savage means fierce.

Ancient Greeks had their version of Kraken. Scylla was a sea monster. Scylla had four eyes. She had six long necks. Each neck had a scary head. Each head had three rows of sharp teeth. Scylla had 12 legs like tentacles. She had a cat's tail. She had four to six dog heads around her waist. She attacked ships. She grabbed sailors with each of her heads.

Many cultures have stories about sea monsters.

Real-World Connection

Kraken has many limbs. Some humans have many fingers and toes. This is called polydactylism. Devendra Suthar lives in India. He has a world record. He has the most fingers and toes. He has 28 of them. He has 14 fingers and 14 toes. Two of his toes are joined. He wears special shoes. He's a carpenter. He works with hammers and saws. He said, "I have to always be careful to avoid the fingers." He doesn't want to cut them off. He thinks his fingers and toes are lucky. People aren't afraid of his extra body parts. Suthar said, "Because of my extra fingers, people here treat me as a celebrity. They come to see me. And the attention makes me feel special. Children laugh when they see me doing funny tricks with my fingers."

Kraken stories started with **Norse** legends. Norse means things from Norway. Norse people were sailors. They saw many things on their sea travels.

Örvar-Oddr was a Norse hero. He was a Viking. He lived in the 13th century. His best friend was killed. He sought revenge. He took his son on a sea trip. He saw islands. He passed through. He looked back. The islands disappeared. It was Hafgufa. Hafgufa is Kraken. It was sent to kill him.

Kraken used to rule the sea. But forces of good pushed it to the ocean floor. It's waiting to rise again!

Örvar-Oddr mistook Kraken for an island.

Did You Know?

- Kraken has also been called Krabben, Skykraken, and "Sea-Mischief."
- Jules Verne featured Kraken in his book. The book's title is *20,000 Leagues Under the Sea*. In the story, a big squid attacks the submarine.
- *Daedalus* is the name of a ship. It encountered Kraken in 1848. Sailors said it was over 60 feet (18 m) long. Sir Richard Owen said they saw a seal. This caused a big fight between Owen and the captain of the *Daedalus*.
- Ichthyosaurs were dinosaurs. They were fish lizards. Scientists found ichthyosaur bones. An ichthyosaur had been squeezed by a large tentacle. Some thought this was proof of a giant squid or Kraken. Ichthyosaurs were 30 feet (9 m) long. It would take a larger sea monster to eat them.
- Giant squids carry ammonia. Ammonia is lighter than seawater. This is why giant squids can float underwater. They can keep steady without swimming. But ammonia tastes bad. Also, when released into the air, ammonia smells like pee.
- Alfred Lord Tennyson was a famous poet. He wrote a famous poem about Kraken. It was called "The Kraken."
- Some stories say Kraken drags humans to its caves. It keeps them alive. It makes them into slaves.
- In 1782, ten British warships disappeared. Pierre Denys de Montfort studied animals. He blamed Kraken for the missing ships. A survivor shared the truth. The ships had been lost in a hurricane. Montfort's reputation was ruined.

Consider This!

Take a Position: Read about other sea monsters. Compare them to Kraken. Which sea monster is the most terrifying? Argue your point with reasons and evidence.

Say What? Kraken has scared sailors for many years. Explain why Kraken was scary to sailors. Explain this phrase: "The tale grows in the telling."

Think About It! Kraken was really a giant squid. What other monsters are really real animals? Why did people make up stories about monsters? Why did they mistake animals for monsters?

Learn More

- Cerullo, Mary M. *Giant Squid: Searching for a Sea Monster*. North Mankato, MN: Capstone Press, 2012.
- Drake, Ernest. *Monsterology: The Complete Book of Monstrous Beasts*. Somerville, MA: Candlewick, 2008.
- McKerley, Jennifer. *The Kraken*. Detroit: KidHaven Press, 2008.
- Newquist, H. P. *Here There Be Monsters: The Legendary Kraken and the Giant Squid*. Boston: Houghton Mifflin, 2010.

Glossary

anchor (ANG-kur) to stick to the ground and stay put

botanist (BOT-uh-nist) someone who studies plants

camouflage (KAM-uh-flahzh) to blend into the surroundings

capsizes (KAP-size-uhz) causes boats to turn over

life span (LIFE SPAN) how long something lives

maw (MAW) the mouth, jaws, or throat of a beast

Norse (NORS) of or related to Norway

origins (OR-ih-jinz) beginnings; where someone is from, how something got started

predator (PRED-uh-tur) hunter

savage (SAV-ij) fierce

tentacles (TEN-tuh-kuhlz) long moving arms with sucking cups

vomits (VAH-mits) throws up

whirlpool (WURL-pool) a hurricane-like water trap

Index

About the Author

Dr. Virginia Loh-Hagan is an author, university professor, former classroom teacher, and curriculum designer. She loves eating calamari but not the tentacles. Tentacles freak her out. She lives in San Diego with her very tall husband and very naughty dogs.